Capperbar

Capperbar

Dick Sullivan

Coracle Books

By the same author:

Prose
Old ships
Navvyman
Undertones

Poetry
Melanie
Morning on the Mountain
The Moon at Midnight

For more about these books, and also work in
progress, readers are invited to visit the author's
website and blog: **www.ageofumber.com**.

ISBN 978 0 906280 11 9

First published as *Nostos 1-7*, 1998⁄9
Second edition, revised and re-titled *Capperbar*, 2003
Third edition, with Preface, 2010

For Mary

Contents

Theology

Addendum

Capperbar

'Show, not tell' is the catchword for poetry these days – describe, present, but don't explain. For everyday emotions it might work but what about mysticism, which is what this book is all about?

Capperbar, written in the late 1990s and early 2000s, now has a companion volume – *Undertones* – which (being prose) is free to both show and tell. In it, low-level, semi-, mild, minor, slight or lesser mysticism is defined as an experience of something deeper than material reality, although on a very small scale. It's an awareness that below the complexity of the everyday there seems to exist something of the utmost importance – clarity, simplicity, unending kindness and, in fact, unendingness itself. It tends to make people bigger and better, expanding and enhancing the inward life, making receivers more fulfilled, giving them a sense of point and purpose, particularly once they're aware of what it is happening to them.

This spiritual experience seems to be outside time and beyond anything seeable by the light of photons – although, paradoxically, photons can open the way to it by revealing the world's beauty Beautiful things – words, music, art, objects, love, landscape – can shut down the mind to allow that mystic insight to well up and occupy consciousness. In the nature of things, it can only therefore be brief and fleeting, though in compensation it can happen each day, sometimes frequently. These moments must be familiar to millions of people even if they're unaware that what they feel is spiritual. That lack of awareness perhaps justifies a Preface to 'tell'. At the same time, for many people this sense of Greatness seems to be permanently out of reach. For them, no amount of either showing or telling is going to be of the slightest use. It's as though they aren't wired for it. An analogy – a poor and imprecise one – could be with colour blindness. Some people can't see a green meadow or a red traffic light because the right rods or cones are missing from their eyes. You can, of course, show a colour blind person a spectroscope to explain the physics via the spikes and troughs on the screen. Here, the analogy breaks down – mysticism is unshowable in this way, and unprovable. Since there are no BSc degrees in the subject, who is qualified to talk about it? Only those who've been there, must be the answer.

For me it all began in the early days of the Second World War in Mardale, in what is now Cumbria, where the Haweswater dam was just being finished. A village of navvy huts had been built on the fellside at Burnbanks, although school for navvy children was in Bampton a couple of miles away down the lane. Wartime schooling began at four and, come snow or shine, we walked those few miles to and fro each day. One morning in the Spring of 1942 we four year olds were taken on a 'nature ramble' on the fells above the school. Up there in the first warm sunshine of the year we came upon a hedge with the briars of a bramble bush black against the sky. To a child it wasn't a bush but a bramble-tree and it induced a sense of joy and uplift verging on ecstasy. That experience has been repeated, sometimes frequently, ever since. Here's a stanza from *Brambletree* (page 34):

> And still the visions never stop.
> Damon the mower must have seen
> Grass in a meadow quite as green
> As lime leaves reflected in the gleam
> Of this all-steel coffee shop.

The coffee shop is 21st century, of course, and Damon is from Marvell. His lines "I am the Mower Damon, known/Through all the meadows I have mown" always invoke profound undertones in me. An undertone is like an aura enveloping words, works of art, ideas or objects, giving them an extra meaning beyond any intellectual understanding, but powerful and life-enhancing for all that. They worked before I was ever consciously aware of them.

Nearer life's end than its beginning, I began to realise that this recurring uplift and sense of expansion was a spiritual thing – different in degree but not in kind from what the great mystics describe. Why was the connection missed? What had masked it? Insufficient intelligence, perhaps, or because it wasn't part of the culture. Empiricism, the English philosophy of doubt, also tends to breed agnosticism, its natural outcome. Together they make the spiritual almost unthinkable, although the unconscious mind has its own way of seeing things and if the two are not in tune there's always a sense of something missing. Something always was missing and the evolution from nameless experience to knowing (or thinking) that it was mildly mystical can be traced in these verses.

The title poem, *Capperbar*, is a narrative one and was adapted from a novel written in the late 1960s, long before I associated these moments with low-grade mysticism. 'Capperbar' was Nelsonic sea slang for something stolen; Capperbar, the man, has been stolen in the sense of being press ganged into the frigate Niobe. I knew he was a misfit on a gun deck, or anywhere else (for *Niobe* read the world), though back in the '60s I didn't know why.

> We have braces now to splice
> In driven salt that flays
> The skin, and spray
> Like splintered ice.
>
> In your hammock hear
> The ship's skin creak;
> Seams gape open wide and leak
> And you are man-shaped fear.
>
> "Do you hear there, sleepers? Save a clew."
> O Capperbar, what have they done to you?

Relief comes only through the things of the earth and the they give of something eternal and unspoken (because unsayable). Here, Capperbar joins a raid on a French warship:

> "Sway out the boats." They clear the booms
> Encased in blackness like a grave –
> And then the ancient softness of the wave.
> Over them *Niobe* looms.
>
> Midnight-black. No moon. Black
> Ship is hidden by black sea and sky.
> Many a man is going to die
> Before the boats are safely back –
>
> *Yet what a pleasant place to be, steeped*
> *In night and an ancient scent of sea.*

In *Undertones*, I speculate that mysticism might be a factor of introversion. (In that book an introvert is defined as somebody inward world is more real than the outward.) Capperbar is, I now realise, an introvert – the reason he's a with no gift for friendship. His mess mates yarn on the deck:

> "Shark," Old Daddy say, "he can't eat me,"
> Showing tattooed crosses on arm and knee.
> "The cross he works just like a charm"
> (Such is the wisdom of the sea).
>
> "I've seen crabs devouring men,"
> Says Yankee Jack. "Jamaica, '94.
> By the Palisades along the shore.
> It was yellow fever time back then."

'What causes yellow fever?' asks Capperbar. 'Why do limes cure scurvy?' He asks questions partly because he has nothing to yarn about, mainly because answers are what he lives for. This, again, might be one of the basic temperaments of lesser mystics – abstract thinkers living inwardly, looking for the answer to the question: "What's it all about, Alfie?"

Capperbar is also portrayed as an empiricist – the philosophy of doubt which says the supernatural is unprovable and therefore of little interest. He collects ideas to explain the world, make it bearable, give it meaning. The poem ends in injustice. Capperbar is falsely accused of mutiny, Court Martialled, and sentenced to hang. (The date isn't specified but it's around 1798, a few months after the great mutinies at Spithead and the Nore.)

The fleet is hove-to off the coast of Spain. At dawn a boat, mounted with a gun in the bow, sets off from each ship. They encircle *Niobe*: at that time a man found guilty of a capital offence at sea was hauled to the fore yard arm and hanged by his own mess mates. The boats were there to ensure that they, and the whole ship's company, didn't baulk at doing their duty. What comfort can his philosophy of doubt now give him? Empiricism emphasises experience and the senses – so use your senses to experience that up-welling of the peace of Eternity which is the gift of the common things of the earth.

> Capperbar, now glory in each sense,
> Feel *Niobe* lift and heave,
> Sense it all before you leave,
> Your last experience.
>
> Note how ochre are the hills,
> How deeply yellow is the sun,
> How glinting is the long sea-run.
>
> ....
> Sun and dust and heat
> Are rising over Spain.
> Boats scatter through the fleet.

Capperbar never knew that, as he waited to die, he was in the presence of the spiritual, the only kind of spirituality open to us. Neither did I, his author, in the 1960s. Nor was there a single flash of insight by which I suddenly realised that this deep inward peace can also be seen as spiritual. It grew slowly. That realisation – slow in reality – was abrupt in print. Another set of verses, *Godfound*, looks at the common things which induce the (putative) Divine; music (ebony and air), art, carp in a pond, sunshine and shade, rain stains on a brick. All these things raise undertones. In *Capperbar* it's also called 'bramblesight', from that original 1942 'brambletree', which sees the fullness at the heart of things. *Godfound* starts with a rebuke, by the poet to the poet, for his previous blindness to the spiritual before going on to list some of the things of the world which induce that surge of insight so briefly but so powerfully. (The frozen ink in the inkstone in the last stanza comes directly from a Zen haiku: the undertones are in the sound of the words, rather than the image – I've never visited a Zen monastery on a Japanese mountainside. Haiku are, or were, specifically designed to induce a mild jolt of mystic insight, via undertones.)

Blind before the behind-the-mind
You stand and see sharp shadows
On a door, and still you fail
To understand.

The peace of place
Is everywhere:
Rain stain on a brick,
Sunshine on a stair,

Sunlight swayed
By shadow and by shade
On pale Palladian walls.

Elysium is in sties
And stone. In dust,
In rust. In that I trust.

Carp arcing in a pond
Can let you see
Glimpses of divinity.

Where then is paradise? Haloing
Sadness, the imprecise. Myopic
Shadows on a wall lift and flicker,
Blur, and fall. Ink is ice in a cold
Ink stone. Meaning's in the overtone.

Or in the undertones, as used here. Not of, course, that any
of this can be proved. Proof no longer matters, particularly
as its opposite is equally unprovable. Doubt itself is
doubtful. Yet in the end no evidence apart from the
experience itself is needed. Why wilfully give up something
life-lifting for something life-lowering for no good reason?

Dick Sullivan,
London, 2010

The Cavern and The Brambletree

Prelude

Capperbar 1

In Gib they're drinking
Blackstrap wine to Lord St Vincent
And St Valentine. But Capperbar

Can't run away from the rocks
Of Camaret. God help us,
God-the-Ghost, upon this Savage

Coast. Rain is raining bright within
The taffrail's yellow lantern light.

Capperbar in sennit hat
Is the antithesis of Jolly Jack.

The pigtailed timoneer
Biting on his quid
Has never had to rid
Himself of fear.

The quartermaster scans the leech,
The long horizon and the skies:
He never looks behind the eyes.

How can they live so unafraid
Of a chain-shot loaded carronade?

Here's a savagery
Not alone of stone
And spray. Hawke

And Howe are in the bay.

Hogged and broken on the shore
Or all a-wallow in a surf
That will not serve
To ride a ship, are men o' war.

Capperbar, you should be tall,
Dawdling with a cricket ball.

"Come inside," Insider said.
But they recoiled. "The flak is sparse
Tonight. (No Bomber's moon.) Cosmos
Is just inside this little room."

"It's a counter-country, traveller free,
Yet here is isolation's ease.
I-less you'll be, in Arcady."

"Of love it is an edgeless pool
Without a single molecule."

"All-deep, it is. All-wide;
Peace without an edge or side
For here there is no space or time."

"It's flowered July in summer rain
Where childhood splendour's come again."

"And in the night the roving Ghost
Will keep you from the rock-thick coast."

"For when the bomber's gone,
And flak has ceased,
You are the chapel and the priest."

Insider II

And yet you're medusa'd into stone
By a letter in a letter box
Or the ringing of a telephone

For Hell, we think, is only this -
A raging mind in its own abyss
While outside in summer shines the sun

(And, no, the moon can't come to grief
Upon the rock of Tenerife.)

Each outing is a losing raid
For the enemy is unafraid,
Unknowing of you all.

How can you evaluate
People in an alien state
Where your alphabet's unknown?

By them of course you're bruised:
The gecko and the ape are fused
And shuffle on a knucklebone.

You cannot read their outerness
And so are fated to distress.

O hairy half-man, what have you done?
Banished peace from underneath the sun.

Outsider

"I am Paul, free in jail…."
No, they crave a story, need a tale.

A brig's becalmed close in to Brest,
Niobe too is all at rest.
Guns are firing from the shore.

The quarterdeck is blown away;
Ivy dangles, red not green,
Where half a dozen men had been.
Boats are on a shot-skimmed sea.

A slatch of breeze, a ruffled tide,
Niobe sidles to her boats,
Pulls them closer to her side.

Sails are slatting, cracking stiff.
She lurches, now set free.
Guns are silent on the cliff.

In all that bending hydrosphere
The captain is defeating fear.
Different far is Capperbar.

Their heads are boxes, all opaque,
Yet normality we're told they are
(All that suiting stretched on hams
Measured now in kilograms)
Unsuited to the stranger Capperbar.

The vicar's not here to preach
Or prate but stumble, matey,
Inarticulate. Arms akimbo, they
Sway in piety and pray.

Why can't they just abide,
With Greaterness inside?

Part One

Glenelg

And then the scent of sea at last
And coffee from the lilac flask
On barnacled and sea-wracked rocks.

The sea is now so full of sun
A surf of light is breaking
On the shore.

Shadows stroke the bulk of Skye.
What else in nature could so caress
That brutal heap of emptiness?

Lying on this headland of the bay
I watch the ferry from Kylerhea
Ply, re-ply, her tide-bent passage
To the Isle of Skye.

Half hidden from the land
Is a little beach among the rocks
Where a soft sea sucks at sand.

Squint through the narrows
At this summer-sequined sea.

What do tides evoke?
Vernon in a grogham cloak:

Sea-white rock of Quiberon
When the light has all but gone:

Swap Manhattan for a nutmeg tree
After one great battle on the sea.

Outside is a rage
Of weather and big seas,
Rain from the nearby Hebrides.

Skirt the sheepfold and the pen
In all that streaming nitrogen.
A redcoat once paraded there,
There by the barrack, workhouse grim:
What, you wonder, became of him?

You were jailed by scenery
In a place that failed. Languid
Talk of sheep by a people half
Asleep. About you everywhere
You took the sadness of despair.

To The Cape

Gargoyle-ridden, I was on my way
From Windhoek to Three Anchor Bay
Down by the Cape with little hope.

White, Malay, and Hottentot
In the melting pot of Rehoboth
Forty years ago. Dust as grey as tow:

Grey grainless dust that clung,
"I, outlander of outlandish tongue."

Sunday, and a wind pump
Screaked. Early heat. Sweat that leaked
In runnels on a dusty face.

A streetless place of haphazard
Shacks. No one turned their
Backs. I was a man of glass
Less visible than the air
Through which I passed.

A girl without a chest
And no attempt
To hide contempt
Slid me a dish, dry as dust,
Of boerewors and drier bread.

Gumboots on a beach:
Each pace was a ripping up
Of roots. A dry white sun
Seemed to spin dust from air
As I stood by the roadside there.

A car trailed dust,
Twin vortices, to trickle
On the trees, drooping,
Waxy, dry. Day drooped
By by the dirt highway.

A truck, dust blasted
Free of rust, pulled up.
Leaning sideways in the back
Was a ramshackle stack
Of beds and tables, chairs
And chests of drawers.

Two sallow lovers sprawled
In intimate embrace;
I, appalled
With reddened face.

Spinning wheels
And whorls
Of spiralling dust.
Open lust.

Kalkrand. Silence from its hub
Spread in a circle wide around
The flattest and most soundless ground.
Railroad track and shacks.
Earth was a hammered disc
Where to run was to run the risk
Of spinning all untethered off.

A loco way out there
Dipped and curtsied in oil-like air
Swelling and shrinking to the beat
Of haze and heat. "Such black smoke,"
Some one spoke. Me.

Rushing dust. A truck
Stopped at the petrol pump.
An eye, a ball of meat,
Fixed me in the heat.
Pointed chin. Pointed crown,
Staring at me up and down.
He spat. A bit of German spit.
Then hit my pack and broke the frame.

A diamond man from the USA
Took me to Springbok. All the way.

Like a CMB we sped
Ahead of our twin wakes of dust
And the disc of world came too.

Hills grew on its farthest rim,
Dim and buckling in the heat;
Heaps of dust, boneless dunes
Not unlike the moon's.

Headlamps like an early frost
Were splashing in the dust,
Or patches of the palest yellow
Flowers, primroses of pure light.
Skin and cloth now deeply sallow,
On we drove into the night.

The Cape was new, new made almost;
Sea broke in spume along the coast,
Everywhere sea broke clean and white,
Air yellow in the morning light.
Everywhere a quiet boom.

I went looking for a room
In a rooming house all dark
Inside; clinker built, an ark
With a shaky belvedere.

A woman, kit-bag-bra'd,
In badly faded purple fard,
Kept watch upon the gangplank there
With promised joys. "I wanna nice
Clean boys." Each room was purple too:
Drapes and bed and purple mat
On lino fading then to blue.
"Six poun' I wanna for dat
Room. One hour, two hour, you come back?"

But there you never did unpack.
What sowing of wild oats
Did you then miss? Instead you went
To stay by crayfish boats and palm
Trees by a bay, that gargoyle
With you all the way.

At The Cape

"I've ruined you," with spite she said.
Crockery shook. She hated nerves.
The waiter sidled back to serve
Steak—in-toast. "You boast
About me, don't you? To your friend?"

Gingham like a frock
Covered tabletop and pane.
The lady ate again,
Sucking cattle grease
From knuckle to the nail.

"I have to marry. Don't you see?"
(Thank God, I think, it wasn't me.)
"David's rich but wants to touch."
(I thought of crayfish boats
Above the beach.) I said:
"I guess in time he'll want his oats."

"You're a thing without a spine"
(And I too thought so at the time).

Fumblingly I paid. Afraid
And flustered, I left too much,
Lacking a common or a kingly touch.

"You left a tip?" "Half a crown."
"You little rubbish, get it back."

Later I wrote it down,
That tale of Juddering Jack
In the oddness of that town.

"Sixpence only you should have left."
Of such small change was life then made,
And palm trees by an Esplanade.

"Where are they gone," you wonder now,
"With wizened skin and wrinkled brow?"
Big ships were steaming from the bay.

A stoker in the hole
Is shovelling Cardiff coal
On a still red-dustered sea.

An empire's in late decline;
Marlin boats with rod and line.

An un-macho Hemingway
Is beached in Durban Bay;
His shadow in the sea
Floats below the clash
Of sun and iron-filing fish.

"I'm on the rocks."
"Where did you hear
That I take bribes?"
"Around the docks."
Angrily he cries:
"Who told you this?"
"I have no friend."
A salt sea hissed outside.

Strip a label with a fingernail;
Pour gas and cold and beer
Into that seething wilderness of fear,
Foot juddering on a rail
In a liner-shaded bar.

"Man! Were you ticking."
In a scent of brandied ice
Is innocence devoid of vice.
"Ja, man, like a bomb."

But what a mess
The day you tried to bribe
A union man by that dockside
And ended eyeless by an altar stone
In a blur of terror, all alone.

Brundisium

Big city in hot July;
Bright hubbub
By the pub
As I stroll by.
What do they talk about
Over bottled beer and stout?

Yet still one day
You hope to come
Wayside stained
To Brundisium?

Ochre holes child-deep in sand
Will not withstand the coming tide.

I'm on a long Victorian street
(A flue conveying heat)
High-stooled within
A coffee shop
Fan-cooled, but hot,
Stirring coffee with a coffee spoon
On an alien summer afternoon
As I note in every wayward face
How undivine's the human race.

Human shoals respond
And shift like mackerel in a tide.
(Don't mind me. I lack the bond
To bind me to mankind,
In fact can barely comprehend
The meaning of a friend.)

Watch a pick up in the park.
Continents collide and part.

All has given way to sex
Which couples, yet disconnects.

Can you now begin to hope
For the acquaintance of a Swift,
The friendship of a Pope?

Not in this Catullan town
Which keeps its pecker up,
Its knickers down.

"Real men are really rude.
We hump and writhe and jug and jump,
Bum working like a suction pump,
You pi-faced prude."

Oh!

The tarmac underneath my feet
Is plasticining in the heat,
Sol-softened for soft-soled men.
Beware that blazing carcinogen.

The canal is summer algal green
But I remember I have seen
It floed with ice. Ice frozen
Into ice like giant lily pads.

On Primrose Hill bipeds prowl
And mate where once a tiger growled
And ate a woolly rhino by the Zoo.

Mankind is milling here in droves;
Did God-the-Logos really cook
Their carbon in his cosmic stoves?

Part Two

Cavern

What is this cavern,
Cosmos-big and of a stone
Unbounded by the bone?

"God," He says, "I think you'll find
In that counter-cosmos of the mind."

Then why do you hide
And fail to fill
The cavity
Inside the hill
If it's better to abide
Gravid with a God inside?

Well, I shall go and sit
Silent by the canyon lip.

A rio grande like a thread
Of white bleached cotton lies below.
Over there corruption's bred,

For all is greed
Amid the cacti
And the locoweed.

Out of your cavern
Please will you bring
A beige guitar
And a gem-rich ring.

In the unflak'd night we talk:
"Ask, and I will give.
Ask, and I forgive."

"I am the Underall and Nethermost,
An island lacking in a coast."

So I at least (at last) have done
With journeys to Brundisium?

"No. You need to come
In friendship to Brundisium."

Then he slips back
Before the daylight's
Rising flak.

Shrewd and raddled, the shire's reeve
Is ambling through the tumbleweed.

Brambletree

And then the scent of beck at last
And coffee from the lilac flask.

Here rock is wrapped in river,
River plays with light.
Note it in despite
Of pity for your plight.

Brown-pooled, rock-floored,
Jam-jarred you could fish
For fish too little for a dish.

Eel trap's gone, I see, but
No one ever caught and elver
That I remember: a timber hut
It was in which to climb
Scented by clean river slime.

In the dug-out Cumberland Ike
Takes his ease with a cutty pipe
Under a dam with a copper
Core. Mardale's marred forever more.

Around here lurks
The Corporation Water Works;
The '30s linger on
In all you look upon.

Millennium on its axletree?
Here is 1943;
Boys with brylcreem'd hair
Em-bus for the picture house

And beer, while Errol Flynn
Has yet the war to win.

Here's the beginning of it all:
Trout-ringed, rain-ringed river,
Midge-itch and cuckoo call.

Brambletree is bramblebush
In a hedge all overgrown.
Hear the wartime bomber drone.

To sense the godhead all you need
Is a mind unminded, brambletree'd.

And still the visions never stop.
Damon the mower must have seen
Grass in a meadow quite as green
As lime leaves reflected in the gleam
Of this all-steel coffee shop.

Godfound

Blind before the behind-the-mind
You stand and see sharp shadows
On a door, and still you fail
To understand.

The peace of place
Is everywhere:
Rain stain on a brick,
Sunshine on a stair,

Sunlight swayed
By shadow and by shade
On pale Palladian walls.

Elysium is in sties
And stone. In dust,
In rust. In that I trust.

Carp arcing in a pond
Can let you see
Glimpses of divinity.

Where then is paradise? Haloing
Sadness, the imprecise. Myopic
Shadows on a wall lift and flicker,

Blur, and fall. Ink is ice in a cold
Ink stone. Meaning's in the overtone.

In frog'n'flop the poet caught
That moment of the loss of thought

For Basho, no one's fool, got
Soppy over petals in a pool
While the moon at midnight
Wowed Li Po with simple gold
And indigo.

A painter's painting in the mind
Things you cannot hope to see,
In blue and lapis lazuli.

Salvation too is given wing
By the physics of a tautened string

And don't forget
Mozart on a clarinet
Is more than ebony
And air.

And the world of course is bramblebright
When seen (alas) by bramblesight

For God-the-Ghost is always nigh:
Watch him with your bramble-eye

And do not ever doubt
Godglory shines about.

If you'd been with God in Rehoboth,
He'd have spared you forty years of wrath;

Ignoring him's the under-sin,
The folly of the Jacobin.

Part Three

Tolmers Square

"All right? Okay? All right?"
Stammers duffle-coated Jack
(The date is still pre-anorak).
"You're right. Shocking cold."
Already she is very old.

"No, Christmas ain't the same.
All the costers used to sing,
Especially after Mafeking."
By gaslight I note it down
Under the hill in Camden Town.

"Weren't the old days bad?"
"A little pony and a trap
For crabs my Granfer had."
"The old days? Weren't they bad?"

"Yes. Them was good old days.
Them winkles come in trays
From the eel shop oppo-sight.
Good old days. You're right."

"My Granny used to send me round
Selling walnuts up in Camden Town.
The old Goat public, to workmen there."

We're pooled in yellow light.
"If the crop was good they'd pay
A shilling a bushel for them hops.
What's he say?" "It's not the same."
"Who's to blame?" "*It's changed.*"
"He's right. I say you're right."

I'm aching on a hardwood chair
In a lino'd room in Tolmers Square,
Fugitive from the old Queen's reign,
Times that never now can come again.

"Pease pudding you could get,
And saveloys." Outside is wet.
"Many of them pies I've ate.
Penny pies from Sweeney Todd,
Him as had the barber shop."

Jack the Ripper, Juddering Jack,
Them days won't never now come back.
"Put on them taters, have you, Ann?
That's good. I say that's good."

Tubers simmer in a pan,
Mantle hisses in its hood.

Navvywoman

Haymaking time, '85,
Swillicking Dick is on the loose
Contemplating how to mooch
A drum of tea, a shive of bread.

In a rutted lane at dusk
White idling smoke he notes.

Rattle of sneck,
Creak of heck:
"Yah bain't ourn!"
Pertly she stares
At the loafer leaning there.

"Dab o' butter? Rib o' beef?
To give a navvy some relief?"

"Who bist thee? Thee bist big!"
"Needful, missus, for to dig
With shovel and with pick."

"Ourn's a carter, gone to town.
Beef ortins? Do sit down."
He takes a clasp knife for a fork.
"Tha's nobbut a bairn to be a wife."

"Where shall yah sleep?" (Growing bold.)
"Under a hedge." "That shall be cold."
"Happen." "Better afore a fire."
"Better in a feather bed."

Not long wed, she blushes pink.
"Pity though I ain't got one."
Her bodice is undone.
"A bolster I can lay atween.
No harm in that." He is keen,
Prising off both boots and hat.

Strong Arm Jack's on Rannoch Moor.
He needs new bluchers and a pedicure.

Moleskin Joe's on a mountainside
Unaware of God or Eastertide.

We're on the edge of Christendom
With a leaky old harmonium.

I meet her off the bus.
Already it's midwinter dusk,
The kind of dismal day that tires
And aches. Midland hunting shires,
All hock deep mud and clay
On this, the shortest day.

A cowl of trees, a hood,
Engulfs us, twin columns
Of deep pain. Mud flows
Like slurry in the lane.

Strings of quiet sleet streak
Across the vale, grey and bleak.
She calls my name and falls,
A memory that still appals.

I drag her on her heels
Under the darkness of a bank,
Clay that feels so cold and dank.

Sleet soaks the greyness
Of her head. That cheap rain
Hood never was much good.

A strain of Victorian pain
Is like a virus in the vein
As she lies dying on the clay
In the darkness of the shortest day.

Love failed a long way back
In some shanty by the line,
A hovel by the track?

No. The epicentre of distress
Is not a woman in a shabby dress:

You were, we think, too blind
To that cavern in your mind.

Ann

Sea-valley and green hillside
Were smelling of river and of tide,
Across the harbour bar
The whole far
World peeled open wide
Into a western sky
Of paint and clarity;
She, a column of content,
I, in torment
By her side.

Below our keel, I knew,
Were wide-eyed wrasse, and weed
Blowing in a tide.

With the Mewstone on the bow,
A breeze began to rise
And I began to doubt
But was, I realize,
Too afraid of fear to put about.

Waves heaped high above our heads.
Seas like hills swooped by;
We were, we knew, about to die.
"Sorry. Sorry," was all I said.

"Poor boy." A hand touched mind.
I'd met the human-and-divine.

Seaton Market

Great-granfer's pony slept
In stables, which have not been kept,
In Seaton Mews, no longer there,
Replaced by glass in Triton Square
Reflecting Annie in her new wheelchair.

Bagel gone, she's supping up
Cappuccino in a Starbuck's
Logo'd pottery coffee cup.

"She was a great believer, I
Do know that. Firmly she believed
And, no, she never was deceived.
He's a good man, God, I think.
A bearded man in a coloured cloak"
("Easy is my yoke"?) "and very kind."

"In churchy pictures that you see
He's always manly, isn't he?
A kindly face that's still unlined.
Promises he will always keep.
Like sheep are people, aren't they? Trot,
Trot, never using any brains they've got."

"You can't pretend they're up to much
And all of them must God offend.
I hope He's there, but who can know?
A nice idea, even so. Something
You need to which to cling
However small or large a thing;"

"Well, to keep you going for a start.
In your heart you say: "Please,
God, help me" when perplexed.
Seaton Market was where we sit."
She is unvexed by a world that's gone.
"Not many now remember it."

"My Uncle Toe was once a beggar here."
"Toe?"
"A mystery how he sank so low."
" But *Toe*?"
"He lost one. In the Army. Long ago."

Paviours are laying paving stones
In the new piazza. "Can you recall
"Where great-grand-daddy had his stall?"
"On the corner near the square.
Somewhere. Somewhere over there."

Now Victorian toughs and toffs
And grime and gas have gone at last;
Lime trees grow in marble troughs
In glass and shining canyons.

The long battalions march away
From Rangoon and Mandalay.

Part Four

St Pancras I

That late summer life was bound
By an engine shed and Camden Town,

For infirmity and age
Had brought us back
To the workhouse
By the railroad track.

Early morning men in hobnail boots
Are blackened by the coal yard chutes.

Here's the workhouse, grimed and grim.
Who could ever worship Him?

Crimson tunic'd they would sit
Jailed in blackened yellow brick.

The all-night locos they could hear,
Slow, with boilers fed, toiling from
The engine shed. And in the rain

And in the shine, wagons rolling
Down the line by that place of pure
Despair. Coal from collier

To smoke in air. Here's the chapel
Where they'd prate of hope. A ha'p'ny
Rate it must have meant to build
To poverty a monument so great.

God at worst (God at best?)
Is a brambletree within the breast?

Millennium

Millennium came. We saw it go
In a fall of rain, a thaw of snow

Countdown

Here's Corelli, crackle-free,
On a keyboard in a small PC;
And here's a ghost half holy.

The alley and its trees are bare
Lit by the city's heartless glare.
Heatless light is soaking up the night.

There in sea-wet Cornish rain
King Harry's ferry on her chain
Cranks herself from bank to bank:

God I know I used to see
In such green tranquillity

And by my metaphoric hearth
In her contented tranquil heart
And a nature almost holy.

Now her brain is ending bit by bit
And there is nothing I can do for it,

Yet the church clock still will chime
When we are free of time

For in the end there has to be
The gift of immortality?

Does the Holy Ghost with me abide
Or shall I wait for Whitsuntide?

Forgive me, Lord, for I'm contrite
In the ice of day, the cold of night.

Cockleshell

To weep for death in age we dare?
Remember *Campbeltown* at St Nazaire

Or the boys of course we never knew
In a canvas cockleshell canoe?

We've lost the battle, and the war,
Accept it as you will, or it deplore,

But can you find in this new pain
The God you thought you'd seen rain?

He's a God of winter's night,
Present in the absent light.

You used to show her what you'd done.
Now Cancer through the signs has run.

Ahead is lying the Madness Pit.
One day soon you'll encounter it.

Comforter

To Newhaven once we used to go
In days of innocence and Jack Cousteau.

Fear of the sea beyond the mole
Ate at entrails, corroded soul,

But she was there to comfort me
In all the cruel terrors of the sea
When the world itself was ocean

And lanyards clattered on their poles
As I lay sleepless in Sleeper's Hole.

Once only can you go to where
The rivers of your Eden flow?

Out there in the sunset west
Was where I thought to find my rest
Wearing summer on my face
Steeped in a poetry of place:

Homesick now I guess I am
For the river up at Morwellham

Or dragging anchor in Looe Bay
Waiting for a tide to take us
To the comfort of a riverside.

Where have you gone, my dear?
To what strange land where
I can never now come near?

I bring you coffee in a plastic cup

But you no longer drink it up.

When she's gone what will I face?
God I fear will not suffice.

Consciousness

Where is the profit in such pain?
What can evolution hope to gain
From such consciousness of grief?

But only God the Maker can explain
Immaterial grief in mattered brain?

Capperbar, you can resist
The humbug of the humanist

For given God there has to be
The gift of immortality.

In the ward is arid air.
She cannot know, and cannot care.

Mind and body cannot mend.
But mind and body cannot end?

Greaterness

There is Venus, evening star,
A natural home for Capperbar
With her sulphuric acid rains
Too near an over-raging sun.
Well, the grieving's partly done.

We know what's coming (it is death)
Through her travail in drawing breath
For those choking coughs of course denote
Brain's loosening grip on throat.

Lonely here it was this afternoon.
Tonight the wireless plays The Tallis
Suite. How pitiless is the Paraclete;

How can he hear you when you pray
So far beyond the Milky Way?

Camden Town

A lightly shaded sun shines down
On all the squalor of Camden Town,

On Cobden on his plinth
In our Victorian labyrinth,
But I have respite for an hour

And am a little free. (As out on bail.)
Old Brown Java's up for sale
In a café with ungilded chairs.

Latte and a coffee cake
Is taken now for craving's sake:
Chocolate I also need. I read

Of death on the farewell page
As one by one the old men go,
A DFC, a DSO,

The skipper of an MTB
Lifting to the swell
In an ancient scent of sea.

Commandos cross the coast. Quietly
They take the life of a soldier
With a knife. Here we are once more
Near Quiberon with Englishmen
On this Capperbarian shore.

Spring-in-winter soon will flow
From out the Gulf of Mexico?

Epilogue

Of what is cosmos
Now composed it not of atoms
As I once supposed? Love's
A word I cannot speak without
Numbed mind or reddened cheek,

Yet what makes a woman about to die
Heed another's stricken cry? "Love,
My love," was her sole reply.

Theology

Godblind

Capperbar, can you think it true
Their fearsome God is fond of you?

Out of the beige bag comes the cat
And you connect their God with that?

Can you talk to him or pray
Among the rocks off Camaret?

God's in the ferry in the rain
But absent where the jack-boots stamp
Inside the concentration camp?

Do they sing on Sirius Three;
"Nearer my greenish God to thee?"

Do they, skinned with greenish slime,
Flap their flippers beating time?
On that planet is one old man
Working out Your Godship's plan?

And who is praying through the night
But a slime-skinned greenish coenobite?

Double Castor's shining on
The little world of Pollux One
Where perhaps they're harkening to
The ITMA Show, circa '42?

Lord, we cry, can there really be
Another poor bugger on Arcturus Three?

And do they keep the faith alive
In the cities of Aldebaran Five?

Ecclesiastic prisons fill
With men the bishop plans to kill.

Baccy for the parson,
Brandy for the squire,
Tyndale for the layman,
Layman for the fire.

For reading English'd Holy Writ
Little Bilney's burned alive
At Norwich in the Lollard's Pit.

The cloaca's in full spate
In Thomas More. He's far
From catholic in his hate.

"Be true hearted unto God,"
Says Tyndale in his Tudor way.
"Faith will save you all one day."

A scaled-down Satan said to Eve:
"Tush, ye shall not die." She'd
Caught the Devil in our first lie.

Then Tyndale met the burning rage
Of a proto-Belgian pre-potatophage.

Horses stamp their iron-shod hooves,
Casting divots with their shining shoes.
The cavalry of God. All that discipline
To chastise sin.

Reason, they say, is passion's slave,
So glass is shivered in the nave.

And all the while the horses' hooves
Break up the turf as if to prove
No man – no God – can now resist
The fury of the fundamentalist.

Soot-black drizzle. Grime.
And then the clocks begin to chime
In a parlour overstuffed.
Dust. Monotony and must.

Better be on Saturn's moons
Than endure those Sunday afternoons.

Prowling over Primrose Hill
A sabre'd tiger caught and killed
A rhino by the palms that grew
Where stand the cages now of London Zoo;
Before, that is, the bear bore down
To feed on berries in Camden Town.

Greenness fills the air and eyes.
I climb that hill for exercise.

Towers not to scrape a sky
But gouge, to scratch, to graze
An eye. Like it if you can,
Brain-abrading Barbican.

Protected by *Romana Pax*
Hob-nailed Roman sandal'd feet
Walked from the Walbrook to the Fleet
Long before St Mary Axe,
Yet all are grave-gripped now.

Saxon Botolph, Celtic Bride,
Were comely by a riverside.

Such little cheer. So much gloom.
Oppression in so large a room;
An altar like an empty stall
Is void of any goods at all.

Yet men rode stone upon the sea
To convert the wild Cornovii,
People of an almost-isle.

Petroc sailed a grinding stone,
(No need of ballast to keep her trim),
God, I guess, accompanied him.

One man rowed a cabbage leaf.
I'd pay to own a bit of his belief.

Gargoyle

Eschatology

It's midsummer in the Med,
A midnight moon is set to shed
Pale light on a ship that's photon-made.

Storm the moonlit mole and cut
With photon-steel and feel a fear-free
Dread. It's not all piety and prayer;

You'll be with Blake at Tenerife
When the Spanish galleons come to grief

While the Spandau hidden in the wood
Will be another bramblebough

And, Capperbar, you shall be tall,
Dandling an iron cannonball.

Heaven to fulfil a need
Will be green and river'd,
Hill'd and sea'd

And the tiger's sabre'd jaw will bite
With canines of purest light.

Gargoyle

The Cathedral Close, and midnight chimed
A dozen cracked uncertain times
On a cold midwinter solstice night
With yellow frost on cobblestones
And pallid sodium light.

67

"Ah!" said Gargoyle. "So you're back?
With chisel and a maul you
Made me on the church's western wall.
If imperfect human art reflects
The workings of the Artifex
Then God and I are surely bad?"

"No," said Simon. "Your sight is blurred.
I cut a Brueghel-ugly imp
But the cobra and the shrimp evolved
Stochastically by rules and chance,
Self-made in this self-making world.
God sent us on a cosmic dance
Yet He, I take it, couldn't know
A limestone imp would in time look down
On all the intrigues of this town."

"There's the bishop," Gargoyle cried.
"Bishop, beneath your fish's head,
Don't you think that Christ is dead?

"You princes of the English church
Have left poor sinners in the lurch."

Empiricist

"How should we live?" said Socrates.
And the answer, then? Not alone
In Plato, God-the-Ghost or Zen.

Agnosticism in a Pope
Is the planet's greatest hope
For the intellect must still insist
On the merit of the empiricist.

And what has God to do with sense?
For us he is experiènced.

Christ

"Was Christ a God?" the Gargoyle said.
"No," said Simon. "I can't think so.
What he did was demonstrate
To Capperbar his fate."

Aquinas

A brig's becalmed close in to Brest.
Niobe too is all at rest.
Guns are firing from the shore.

Capperbar-at-ease-at-rest
Is cool to gods. Capperbar-off-Brest
Cries in anguish for some Greaterness.

Infantry too have often found
God in a foxhole in the ground.

Addendum

Insider III

Who freed Dido into Dis?
A god, we say, should do more than this

For there *is* a cosmos in the head
Of a few (perhaps) like Capperbar
(From Sirius Two we think they are)
Who are alone-yet-unalone
In a cavern bigger than the bone;

There are rude mechanicals and then
There's Hamlet and there's Origen.
Plato-Paul were also Inside men.

No brain or larynx can express
Its oddly filled up emptiness.
It is whereof we cannot speak,

Yet to ourselves we're bound to talk.
Samphire gatherers on the chalk
Evoke in us the Paraclete

Though what He is we cannot say.
Outsiders turn the other way.

Quakerman

Coxery, linguister to his mates,
Was lading herring for the Straits.
Lion's Whelp or *Sparrow Pink*,
To become a Quaker, don't you think,
Is a folly on which you'll sink?

Like flukes of air, catastrophe
Beats upon a user of the sea.
But a Quakerman can't doff a hat
To painted saint or, come to that,
Fire a gun. Yet in the Trade
A man is paid to kill,
Think of killing what you will.

"God is not in steeple house
Or book but in the soul. Look.
Just look." I do and soon I see
An everlasting brambletree.

Coxery too was in love's soft grip,
God-taken from a meaner fellowship.

Sea Bramble

Glint or glisten?
Listen to the sea's
Soft spill of breath.

Louis d'or or new doubloon
Sparkling in the afternoon,
Each wave's a spill of coin.

Where are the old colonials
Chaired in wickerwork and cane?
You'll never see their likes again.

Out there in the raging west
Is still the great blockade of Brest
And red-haired Drake's in God's Name Bay,
Half a Tudor world away.

Salvation is a sun-glazed
Sea, and all those hazed
And salt-caked days.

We round Hurst Point
On a milk-pale sea,
Cool but hot-about-to-be.

By compass rose we make a run
In the raging splendour of the sun
Across Lyme Bay
By Portland Bill
On a sea too still
To wet the shingle
On the beach.

Each pebble's graded by the sea,
But not today. No stone scrapes.

Kelp wrack drapes
Eroded rock with straps
Of coagulated sea

As we sail into a sea scent,
And a sea light. Port is a rent
In rock still hot from the sun,
And then a Cornish night.

St Enodoc

Drink a polystyrene cup of tea
By Padstow and a troubled sea.

Over there is Lyonesse
Where Bedivere took the brand
Excalibur in a knightly hand

For the king, they say, had gone
To the apple isle of Avalon.

Dunes break slow and soft,
Crested like arrested waves,
Upon the bedrock of Bray Hill;
They move yet look so still.

The church of Enodoc
Is founded not upon a rock
But in a hollow dune.

Lichen, like yellow paint,
Is stippled on a wall. Feel
The nearness of the saint?

God-the-Ghost is rain-wet bark
And evening coming on. And dark.

St Mawes

A sentry with unbarbered hair
(Arquebus upon a knee)
Dozes in sight and sound of sea,

While soldiers in slashed shoon
Idle away a Tudor afternoon

For a Tudor light stills falls
Time-stilled on Tudor walls;
No clocks tick
By walls a fathom thick.

Granite is underfoot and under
Hand. Little is here to understand
But all to feel-'n'-know.

In this pocket Elsinore
Young Hamlet can mature.

Cornwall

A brook is trickling though
Palm and fleeced bamboo,
Flickering over sand
To a very Cornish sea.

A fishing port of painted stone
Is stacked around its rocky cove.
What pirate man from Spanish Main
Sheltered here from Cornish rain?

Fish cellars fill with fish.
Pilchard is a common dish,
Altering the colour of the sea.

What flat-nosed Bedford drove
Along this wartime concrete road
With slitted lights?

A pillbox squats
With ivy-circled
Machine-gun slots.

Look out on 1941
Along the barrel of a gun.

Gaze at 1942
And a river oddly blue.

We're by the bay with older eyes
But being now no longer sings
To a gull with wind-bent wings.

By waysides rich, unbotanised,
(The scent, the sight, was what I prized)
A boy with weightless feet
Was stepping out to meet
Eternity.

I used to wait for time to pass,
Now the sea and I are wrinkled up
And an alien's in the looking glass,
A man from Sirius Three
Bearded white with shaving foam
And a million million miles from home.

Egg-rich diet, clotted cream,
Flitch of bacon on a beam,
Gone's the place we used to know
One exchange of genes ago.

1956

Write a threnody
For what has ceased to be:
That altered look
Of country under snow,
Spinney and silt-grey brook
Flowing now so long ago.
Thanksgiving time when
Holly's rimmed with rime
And all is pale with mist
And frost. Dew condenses
Barbed as ice on fences,
Bristling on a rail,
Bucket-shaped in pail.

Under foot's the creak of snow.
Black mid-winter's bright
With snowlight in the night.
Lying on a flock-filled bed
You wait to live before you're dead.

Then hot summer's here again,
Hill idle in the heat. There's
A vacancy on the garden seat
And none to welcome rain.

Rented soil that once uplifted
An agèd man is green with weed.
Contentment's never guaranteed.

Yet there's still that scent of currant leaves,
That itch of summer after rain,
Rain on rhubarb. Rain on grain.

Strutting crow,
Coulter-beaked,
A bit of night
That leaked
Into this bright morning.

Paintings, RA

The gallery is icebox cold
(This cool summer warmed the sea
In time to heat the Equinox)

So let's make a start,
Staring at refrigerated art.

In a cavern, cavern-black,
A lemon on a putty plate
Fixes lobster's swirling claw
With a citric acid look of hate.

The lobster, in splendid lobster-red,
Sprawls more ashamed than boiled and dead.

It's the painter's early phase:
A jug's thick oil, all bluish white,
Is better than the potter's glaze.

Pink and oyster-pink and urine-yellow,
Crimson-red and blue-grey-blue,
Palm-bole brown as no palm is,
A jar an eye can just see through,

While along Iona's rock-bit strand
No one sails or strolls, or lands
From that tranquil turquoise-coloured sea.

At a keyboard in an orange dark
A player's playing JS Bach.

Madam, posing in saffron gown,
Death's already got you down. No
Allure remains in flesh-bare bone.

Not just lipstick but your face
Is smudged. At what moment
Was the Reaper's elbow nudged?

A milliner in oyster-pink
Gazes out of paint that never blinks.

Below the pinkness of the paint,
She ain't prudish. That she ain't.

Here they celebrate in art
The continuity of the tart.

Up from Sussex, down from Herts,
They don't know or seem to care
What's brewing up in foreign parts.

Tea is drunk. Boredom's re-begun
Not long before the fury at Verdun.

Nineteen nineteen Galloway,
Your tranquil towns must hold, in truth,
A platoon or two of shell-shocked youth.
Your hills are much too far away.

If you could only shrink and crawl
Through that gilded portal on the wall
You'd rise in a place that's solely sight.

Does the Norman-archèd door
Open on a grand celestial shore?

At the Abbey, pigment's caught
That moment of the loss of thought

And you realise with sharp dismay
That nineteen-twenties' one-off day
Is out of reach. You can't go where

Post-war fashion pulls cloche hats
Hard down on pre-war skulls.

National Gallery

Here we see much more,
Handed eyes at the lintel of the door.

Here's a swatch of yellow corn,
Milled and floured, baked and gone.

Appeal of apples un-apple green,
Pears of a colour never seen,
Earthenware in grey-blue-lavender.

Note the vacancy in the face
Of a nun who lost her faith
But who yet clings with peasant hands
To a rosary she no longer understands.

See the Godhead, like a saint,
In a splotch of yellow paint.

A guide grips her bosom to enthuse
In a language not many people use.
She too can clearly see
Cypress burning like a brambletree?

But Titian shows what faith can do.
A boy, wine-flask on his hip,
Implores the holy fellowship
And stillness wrapped in Mary-blue.

St Paul

Perhaps the postman soon will call
With another letter from St Paul
For the answer that you seek
Is not in Attic but in koine Greek?

For years your domicile
Was by an oil-thick river of black bile
Though no one chooses, none decides,
To dwell by a river of the suicides:

Turn you then from Plato unto Paul
(On roots his rain will surely fall)
And hope the time is coming when
You join the faith-enrightened men.

St Pancras II

St Pancras, once a spa,
Is now a bit of capperbar. Some
Bugger robbed us of a river.

A legion's camped upon The Brill
Below St Pancras on this hill.

Unsewered Fleet is pouring south
To a Roman harbour at her mouth,

While the 20th in their camp
Are ague-ridden, damp,
Circled by an alien stream.

Unalien though to me.
I could always meet
The seldom-present Paraclete
If the Fleet were only free
And three feet wide.

Tell me, Three-in-Three,
Will One-in-Three suffice
To lead a soul to Paradise?

Yet we no longer call for proof.
Rain will do. Or lichen on a roof.

Fiddler's Green

Crossing sweeper, besom-broomed,
Sits in a garden on a plinth,
Sad in the city's labyrinth.

Four o'clock in a fading light
That hasn't failed. Night
Does not assail with quite
The terror of no-longer days.

Honour sea and all that's been
On your way to Fiddler's Green.

Seaside

Sun block cream and hat,
Lilac coffee pot. All that
And sunlight glinting on a sea.

See the ochre sand of summer,
Sea swept,
Sea wet,
Stretching away
By a sand-scarfed bay.

What delight it would be
To be unique in unscuba'd sea;
Creep of coral, coil of lime,
Sea laps. Lapse of time.

An August sun still smoulders
On waves drooping now like tired shoulders.

Out there's the sparkle of a sea:
Here, a fathom deep, is eternity.

Rye

From the battlements look down
On an elongated river leaving town
In a blue-mud groove;

Look across to Dungeness
Over the town's unevenness
And rooves so Roman-red.

On the knoll (forget the sea)
Is literature, gentility;
The Jameses here are on the list –
The novel-writer, the Pragmatist -
And the bishop's boy
At the turning of the lane
Before the night the Heinkels came.

Cobbles ripple like a rill
Back through time and down the hill;
Palm-big bricks are russet red,
Monuments to the unnamed dead
In this time unevened town.

French youth go nasalling by.
What brings them all to Rye?
Let them too depart in peace.

The church, not broad perhaps but wide,
Is close against the once-seaside;
Golden leopards are tailed with ships.

The old church clock and its pendulum
Tick you on to Kingdom-Come.
By the Quarterboys a quote
Truly warns that life is brief
But I, who've had enough of grief,
Button up my coat and think of tea.

Soon be summer. What will it add
To the thousand years this town has had?

Life has gone. There was no plan
But now I've paid the ferryman.

Capperbar

Capperbar II

A fat white weevil's in the biscuit
Barge. *Niobe* now is sailing large,
Heading for the great blockade.
Capperbar sits slewed, afraid.

Gundeck's raining, reeking, dim;
What of comfort can we say to him?

No contentment's here. No woman's thighs.
It's better when desire dies.

All winter long we'll see no sun
And the war has twenty years to run.
Bare poles wag leafless against the sky.

"Out or down, lads. Out or down.
You're a long way now from Plymouth town."

"Our ships have ringed the western sea
And closed the coast of Brittany."

Long Atlantic rollers sweep,
Depriving men of rest or sleep,
Bursting in the Roads of Brest.

We're in bewitchment's grip.
Eight bells. The long night watch
Begins. Feel the long Atlantic fetch
Lift and pitch each groaning ship.

Stinking burgoo, butter's rancid lumps,
Nightlong labour at the pumps.

We have braces now to splice
In driven salt that flays
The skin, and spray
Like splintered ice.

Prowling corporals creep and probe. "Dowse
That glim." Snow is warmer than the rain
That frees the rigging once again.
"Do you hear there, sleepers? Rouse."

In your hammock hear
The ship's skin creak;
Seams gape open wide and leak
And you are man-shaped fear.

"Do you hear there, sleepers? Save a clew."
O Capperbar, what have they done to you?

We're standing into Plymouth Sound
From Penlee Point to Cawsand Bay.
"Bumboats, sir, and women on their way."
Soon they're swarming all around.

Rum or ale's for sale, and women too.
Now, Capperbar, what will you do?

Let me tell you this once more,
You cannot even step ashore
Because the Navy tells you so.

Accept with grace this little lull
For encapsulated in this hull
Is certainty,

A certainty you cannot flout
For all your philosophy of doubt.

"Who goes there?" the guffy shouts.
Your philosophy of doubt
He cannot share,

While the smack of a half-spent musket shot
Is sure to make your shoulder blade grow hot.

Undoubtingness you may deplore
But the Captain reads his certainty
In the Articles of War.

The bosun's mate takes up the whip
As a silence settles in the ship.

Pain is everywhere: in eyes, in hair,
Everywhere but in your back.

The second stroke will break the skin,
The open wound of discipline.
Your back is ridged for life.

The Captain's pig-and-chicken farm
Is by the Sick Bay in the bow
Where Capperbar lies broken now
With only vinegar for balm.

Mr Price, a doctor in a periwig,
Wipes brandy from his lips;
Veteran of a dozen ships,
He's oblivious of the squealing pig.

"Good case of ship fever, over there.
Burning up with petechiae."
He fixes his only eye on Capperbar.

"The loblolly boy will wash his feet
To dissipate the heat
But he very soon will die."

"No hope for him, I say.
He's glowing like a galley stove.
Over board's where he'll be hove
If we ever leave this bay."

"What's that bloody din?"
His messmate's tumble in,
Already stupefied:

Old Daddy, Yankee Bray,
Young Davy, small Benny May.

Yankee grips a leather can.
"Capperbar, you'll take a swig?"
(The pig is squealing for its swill.)
"You took your flogging like a man."

They've all been drinking hard.
"Purser's swipes it ain't."
Pure brandy then, with just a taint
Of tar. "Smuggled in a ball of lard."

"Masthead! Where away?"
"Larboard beam. Across the bay."
"Get an offing. Wear the ship.
Tonight there'll be a little trip."

"Sway out the boats." They clear the booms
Encased in blackness like a grave,
And then the ancient softness of the wave.
Over them *Niobe* looms.

Midnight-black. No moon. Black
Ship is hidden by black sea and sky.
Many a man is going to die
Before the boats are safely back.

Yet what a pleasant place to be, steeped
In night and an ancient scent of sea.

A following sea, an easy ride,
And then the loom of the frigate's side
And a broadside's roaring overhead.

Red cutter reaches the starboard bow:
Adrenalin will disallow
All fear. Follow the Gunner, Mr Cash,
Over the cathead to cut and slash,
Lit by no lantern but the flash
Of guns. With boarding pike
Young Davy stuns and kills, godlike
Unaware of death. Yankee strikes
With every breath. Gunfire shines,
Staining hull and rigging red,
Blazing on the newly dead.
Human tubing hangs like vine.
Capperbar, you're head to head
With a red-haired Celt;
Pull a pistol from your belt
And shoot him dead.

It's darker now. Battle's done;
The gunners all are dead. Gone
With them is the fire that shone
In a blaze of gunlight like the sun.

"You there, idler, don't just stand
Idle on a blood-slicked deck,
Another gaping cut upon your neck,
Red cutlass in your hand,"

"Get us under weigh."
O Capperbar, so raw and scarred,
True seaman now of the afterguard.
"Our prize? Cash beyond our pay."

Capperbar III

Here's the Purser, Mr Jones:
The belly in his lap
Is hanging from a thick fat-strap.
I don't believe he's built on bones;

He's growing fatter every day
On food he's paid to give away.

Make chowder in your iron pot;
Fatty pork
And share of shark
And dough with water from the scuttlebutt.

Peg-leg Bandy is the Cook.
"Stew this, sir?" "What's that you say?"
"One tot, sir? Payable Saturday?"
He stows it in his stove with one black look.

Chowder's good. Cheese is rank;
No wonder the Purser's office stank.

The talk now turns to other things to eat:
"Soft tommy and sausage."
"Murphies and cabbage."
"Bacon. Egg."
"Leg
Of lamb."
"*Ham*!"
But not off Brest in the vanguard of the fleet.

"Shark," Old Daddy say, "he can't eat me,"
Showing tattooed crosses on arm and knee.
"The cross he works just like a charm"
(Such is the wisdom of the sea).

"I've seen crabs devouring men,"
Says Yankee Jack. "Jamaica, '94.
By the Palisades along the shore.
It was yellow fever time back then."

"Inches deep we buried them
And crabs just dug them up again.
Dug them from their shallow graves."

"What causes it?" asks Capperbar.
"The reek of vegetation in the night."
"Nothing cures it?" "No, that's right."
Creak of ship and reek of men and tar.

"It did for us, that yellow jack."
"We lay too close to land."
"Skin as yellow as the sand
We laid them in." "Your sick is black."

Young Davy says: "That yellow jack!
Only fifty of us left
That isle." He looks bereft.
"The Gunner brought us back."

Time to sit and think.
"What's in lemon and in lime
That cures the scurvy every time?"
Grog time, now. Time to sit and drink.

Then to Plymouth once again
To take in stores and quotamen.

One's a Cockney, Henry Blair,
All bare tendons, lean and quick,
Whippy as a withy stick
Or high-strung whippet with a hare.

"As a follower of Paine
You'll have everything to gain."

"Freight balloons will fill the air
Along with ships that steam and glide
Into the wind. They're on the Clyde
Right now. We're almost there."

"Think how things will surely be
When this old world's in smithereens –
Fat mechanics floating in machines
And no poor sailormen at sea."

"Think about *this*, then:
Work half a day
For a full week's pay
And live like gentlemen."

"All these things can surely be
With just a little mutiny."

Flynn is sailing by another chart,
Swearing-in young Irishmen
With a cross above the heart.

"The King of England, Mr Guelph,
Is as mad as any addled dub
While Florizel, his elder cub,
Thinks only of himself."

"Who can then explain to me
Why they're the rulers of my country?"

In a dotted line of shade and sun
Men with neckerchiefs above their ears
Are standing to each gun;

103

Eighteen pounders, buff and grey,
Each sharply lit by one square ray.

Sea speckles the deckhead beams.
Niobe's creaking in her seams.

Listen to the ripple of the sea.
Stern window's gone,
Got by one French gun.

See the Frenchman's billowing sail
And her tar-black martingale
Sharp against the glisten of the sun.
"Fire at will." Put linstock to the quill.

Let go the tacklefalls;
Sponge, cartridge, wad and ball.

Trucks grumble up against the sill,
Smoke coils, pink with flame,
Stopping us from taking aim.

Wad and ram, ram and ball,
Tail on the tacklefalls and haul.

Lilac gun smoke's on the sea.
"Alive, are we?" "What?" "Hurt?"
"Alive, I think. Just caked in dirt."
Young Davy's lost his knee.

"You there, idlers, on your feet.
Sweep away the shambles and the reek,
Disregard the shriek of men."
Pigs root for human meat.

Young Davy's on the orlop, dim
And dark. He doesn't beg.
By candlelight light he'll lose his leg.
What of comfort can we say to him?

Rain is falling through a kinder night.
It's three o'clock, or seven bells.
Lookouts call that all is well.
South we're heading now for Spain.

Powder splutters. There's a shot.
In the flash we see the face of Flynn,
That misbegotten Jacobin.

His rebellion has begun:
He's killed the sentinel
With a small handgun.

Bayonets briefly glisten red.
The Captain at his cabin door
Is calm amid the ship's uproar.
Three more mutineers are dead.

Flynn quickly now turns cat-in-pan
And grips poor Capperbar. "Your man,
Sir, here's your man. He fired the shot
That killed the sentry on the spot."

Capperbar, there's nothing you can do.
The fleet's hove-to outside Cadiz;
Court-martial time it is for you.

After the mutiny at Spithead
They need a body lying dead
And it doesn't matter who.

"Did this book inspire your plan?"
"Sir, it is not mine."
The Captain has been lavish with the wine.
"It's called *The Rights of Man*
And was found within your kit.
You must surely know of it?"

"I'm a printer, sir, from near Liskeard."
We hear a snort
(The Admiral is suffused with port).
"You're a seaman in the afterguard."

A rising sun, a Cyclops's eye,
Will watch you as you die.

Boats set out from all the ships.
In each a gun
Is glinting in the sun.
Niobe curtsies now, and dips.

Capperbar, now glory in each sense,
Feel *Niobe* lift and heave,
Sense it all before you leave,
Your last experience.

Note how ochre are the hills,
How deeply yellow is the sun,
How glinting is the long sea-run.

Niobe now is ringed by boats,
A mouth with teeth that floats
And threatens yet to bite.

Your neck will never break. You'll choke
As they hoist you like a flag
Through the death-gun's yellow smoke.

Sun and dust and heat
Are rising over Spain.
Boats scatter through the fleet.